All You Need Is Faith

PEDRO WILSON

ISBN 978-1-0980-8107-2 (paperback)
ISBN 978-1-0980-8108-9 (digital)

Christian Faith Publishing, Inc.
832 Park Avenue
Meadville, PA 16335
www.christianfaithpublishing.com

Printed in the United States of America

When going through a difficult time in your life, don't stop or quit moving forward. Have faith; God might be changing you not your circumstances.

When bad things happen, it's not always due to you doing something wrong. There is purpose to your pain; just remember God has not left you. Certain things in our lives have to happen for us to grow.

Have confidence to move forward in life because of the proof that God is always with us when we stand or fall. Courage is moving forward from fear. Don't let fear rule your life. Be willing to be wrong just to find out to be right. Stop worrying about what you don't have. Thank the Lord for what you do have.

> Do not be anxious about anything, but in every situation, by prayer and petition, with thanksgiving, present your requests to God. And the peace of God, which transcends all understanding, will guard your hearts and your minds in Christ Jesus. (Philippians 4:6–7 NIV)

> The fear of the Lord is the beginning of wisdom, and knowledge of the Holy One is understanding. (Proverbs 9:10)

We must have faith that the Lord will answer our prayers after praying.

> God in heaven, give me the patience for others. Help me to love others. Help me to love them and forgive them as you have loved

and forgiven me. Give me the wisdom to speak the truth when others are going astray. Give me the words to speak by leading me with the Holy Spirit. Restrain me when I am tempted to speak the truth for my own selfish gain. Thank you for your love. In Jesus's name. Amen.

2

No matter what you don't have as long as you have God in your life, you have more than people who don't have God in their lives.

The truest way we express our love is through our actions not words. Our actions reflect what's in our hearts and thoughts. Think of your actions, do they speak of love, or are they contrary to God's love?

Sometimes the things that hurt you the most teach you the greatest lesson in life.

Don't sacrifice your future based on the bad things that happened in the past.

Don't try to change people. If they won't change for God, they won't change for you. A person will only change for the better if they want to. Pray for them and move forward; don't let them take your joy and faith.

Proclaim it with strength: God, I will praise You, for I am fearfully and wonderfully made; marvelous are Your works, and that my soul knows very well.

Loving God is not just what we think in ourselves. We can be the most loving people in our minds, but if all we are practicing is hatred, then we are no better than liars. A person who hates his or her brother or sister in Christ is a liar because they claim to love God when they actually don't. Loving God is about how you treat everyone around you, not just in the declarations you make about how loving you think you are.

Blessed is the man that endureth temptation: for when he is tried, he shall receive the crown of life, which the Lord hath promised to them that love him. (James 1:12)

Enjoy where you're at, and know you are not where God wants you to be yet.

> A little that a righteous man hath is better
> than the riches of many wicked. For the arms of
> the wicked shall be broken: but the Lord uphold-
> eth the righteous. (Psalm 37:16–17)

3   Are you in a crisis today? That means God is up to something! You're about to be changed. You don't have to stay the same. God is getting ready to make a change in your life.

Know that no matter what, God has you covered. He will keep you at rest. He will strengthen you, and He will see you through the tough times. Know that in everything you do, the trials that come your way and the challenges you face, there is no need to worry nor fear; the Lord is with you at all times.

> Have not I commanded thee? Be strong
> and of a good courage; be not afraid, neither be
> thou dismayed: for the Lord thy God is with thee
> whithersoever thou goest. (Joshua 1:9)

Fear is something you feel not something you should run from. God says, fear not for I am with you.

The love that we show each other will strengthen our bond in the faith and encourage more people to come to God.

> The wise man looks ahead. The fool
> attempts to fool himself and won't face facts.
> (Proverbs 14:8)

> Now I beseech you, brethren, by the name
> of our Lord Jesus Christ, that ye all speak the
> same thing, and that there be no divisions among
> you; but that ye be perfectly joined together

in the same mind and in the same judgment.
(1 Corinthians 1:10)

When you don't understand what's happening in your life, just close your eyes, take a deep breath, and say, "God, I know this is your plan. Just help me through it."

> Teach me to do thy will; for thou art my God: thy spirit is good; lead me into the land of uprightness. (Psalm 143:10)

4   You cannot be selfish and humble at the same time.

Don't let shame keep you tied to the past. Some emotions are so destructive, so damaging, so hurtful, and so noneffective that the only thing you can do is change it. You've got to change what you're feeling. If you want to succeed in life, you must learn how to master your moods. When you're dealing with an emotion that's holding you back, you've got two options: you either change it or you direct it.

> Commit to the Lord whatever you do, and He will establish your plans. (Proverbs 16:3)

Our tears say prayers that our words don't say.

> Yet if any man suffer as a Christian, let him not be ashamed; but let him glorify God on this behalf. (1 Peter 4:16)

> In God I will praise his word, in God I have put my trust; I will not fear what flesh can do unto me. (Psalm 56:4)

> O give thanks unto the Lord; call upon his name: make known his deeds among the people. (Psalm 105:1)

God closes doors to protect us and redirect us.

> Search me, O God, and know my heart: try me, and know my thoughts: And see if there be any wicked way in me, and lead me in the way everlasting. (Psalm 139:23–24)

> For all the law is fulfilled in one word, even in this; Thou shalt love thy neighbour as thyself. (Galatians 5:14)

5   I would rather fail doing something I love than succeed in something I hate.

Not all suffering is from sin. The Bible says sometimes suffering is according to the will of God because God is more interested in your character than your comfort.

> The just man walketh in his integrity: his children are blessed after him. (Proverbs 20:7)

> Every way of a man is right in his own eyes: but the Lord pondereth the hearts. (Proverbs 21:2)

> Blessed are they that keep his testimonies, and that seek him with the whole heart. (Psalm 119:2)

Everyone wants to be heard but has nothing to say.

Keep your eyes on God. If you focus on your problem, you're going to be distressed and depressed. If you focus on God, you're going to be at rest.

God knew before you were born that you would be reading this in this moment. He planned to get your attention for just a few seconds so he could say this to you: I've seen every hurt in your life, and I've never stopped loving you. You matter to me. I love you more than you will ever know. I made you to love you, and I've been waiting for you to love me back.

> Therefore the Lord himself shall give you a
> sign; Behold, a virgin shall conceive, and bear a son,
> and shall call his name Immanuel. (Isaiah 7:14)

Father, thank You for the things that You have prepared for those who love You. I love You with my whole heart. And I pray that today, Your Spirit, which is a Spirit of revelation, shows and reveals to me these things that are prepared in advance. I want to receive them, and I will because I know that You want the best for my life! In Jesus's name, amen.

> For I reckon that the sufferings of this pres-
> ent time are not worthy to be compared with
> the glory which shall be revealed in us. (Romans
> 8:18)

God wants you to remember that He is faithful and always present with you, and nothing could ever change that. He was, is, and always will be your Father.

You need to live for an audience of one: God. That's Jesus's path to complete and total joy. He said,

> I have told you this so that my joy may be
> in you and that your joy may be complete. (John
> 15:11)

> But seek ye first the kingdom of God, and
> his righteousness; and all these things shall be
> added unto you. (Matthew 6:33)

> There is none holy as the Lord: for there is
> none beside thee: neither is there any rock like
> our God. (1 Samuel 2:2)

A righteous man of God would offer a weary traveler a bed for the night and invite him to share a quiet conversation of the Lord over a bowl of soup.

It's not about anger; it's about peace. It's not about power; it's about grace. It's not about knowing your enemy; it's about knowing yourself.

Storms may rage, but they are but for a moment. Your God's favor is for life!

> The Lord shall fight for you, and ye shall hold your peace. (Exodus 14:14)

> He that followeth after righteousness and mercy findeth life, righteousness, and honour. (Proverbs 21:21)

> What shall we then say to these things? If God be for us, who can be against us? (Romans 8:31)

> I will praise thee, O Lord, with my whole heart; I will shew forth all thy marvellous works. (Psalm 9:1)

> O Lord, thou art my God; I will exalt thee, I will praise thy name; for thou hast done wonderful things; thy counsels of old are faithfulness and truth. (Isaiah 25:1)

> Because thy lovingkindness is better than life, my lips shall praise thee. Thus will I bless thee while I live: I will lift up my hands in thy name. (Psalm 63:3–4)

People may not remember what you said but will remember how you made them feel.

Love a person for the way they are not the way you want them to be.

Thanks be unto God for his unspeakable gift. (2 Corinthians 9:15)

But thanks be to God, which giveth us the victory through our Lord Jesus Christ. (1 Corinthians 15:57)

Now therefore, our God, we thank thee, and praise thy glorious name. (1 Chronicles 29:13)

For the grace of God that bringeth salvation hath appeared to all men, teaching us that, denying ungodliness and worldly lusts, we should live soberly, righteously, and godly, in this present world. (Titus 2:11–12)

Be not deceived; God is not mocked: for whatsoever a man soweth, that shall he also reap. For he that soweth to his flesh shall of the flesh reap corruption; but he that soweth to the Spirit shall of the Spirit reap life everlasting. (Galatians 6:7–8)

For the earth shall be filled with the knowledge of the glory of the Lord, as the waters cover the sea. (Habakkuk 2:14)

Walk in wisdom toward them that are without, redeeming the time. Let your speech be always with grace, seasoned with salt, that ye may know how ye ought to answer every man. (Colossians 4:5–6)

> He that keepeth his mouth keepeth his life: but he that openeth wide his lips shall have destruction. (Proverbs 13:3)

Courage is contagious. You never know how many people will join you until you courageously step out in faith.

If we chase God, *His* blessings will chase us.

> Walk with the wise and become wise, for a companion of fools suffers harm. (Proverbs 13:20)

> Verily, verily, I say unto you, He that heareth my word, and believeth on him that sent me, hath everlasting life, and shall not come into condemnation; but is passed from death unto life. (John 5:24)

We must feed our faith with the promises of God.

> May the grace of the Lord Jesus Christ, and the love of God, and the fellowship of the Holy Spirit be with you all. (2 Corinthians 13:14)

Don't be ashamed of who you are. Don't apologize for existing! Instead why not choose to thank God for who you are?

You are absolutely unique, and no one else but you can be *you*! Learn to appreciate yourself as you are with your strengths and even your flaws! Yes, because what God is perfecting in you is an opportunity for Him to support and transform you by His Spirit.

The challenge for us is twofold: We must not allow others to make us feel negatively about ourselves. But we also must make sure that we do not make others feel inferior to us. Treat others like the children of God as well. It's not about being superior; it's about being godlike.

Sadly, people will often try to make you feel inferior for a variety of reasons: to make themselves feel superior, to win, or out of fear of being judged themselves. But God claims each of us as his very own. You are not inferior. You are a child of God, and no one has the right to treat you any other way!

> Wherefore thou art great, O Lord God: for there is none like thee, neither is there any God beside thee, according to all that we have heard with our ears. (2 Samuel 7:22)

> Wherefore, my beloved brethren, let every man be swift to hear, slow to speak, slow to wrath. (James 1:19)

> And let the peace of God rule in your hearts, to the which also ye are called in one body; and be ye thankful. (Colossians 3:15)

*B*ought by the blood of Jesus
*L*iving in His victory
*E*stablished in faith
*S*aved from the curse of sin, despair, depression, and death
*S*ecure in the knowledge of His forgiveness and faithfulness
*E*xpectant that good things will happen today
*D*elivered to bring deliverance!

> But to do good and to communicate forget not: for with such sacrifices God is well pleased. (Hebrews 13:16)

> Even a fool, when he holdeth his peace, is counted wise: and he that shutteth his lips is esteemed a man of understanding. (Proverbs 17:28)

Simply put, a life without Christ has no worth. It means eternal death and damnation. Knowing Christ brings righteousness.

> Now the Lord is that Spirit: and where the Spirit of the Lord is, there is liberty. (2 Corinthians 3:17)

> A man's heart deviseth his way: but the Lord directeth his steps. (Proverbs 16:9)

> I will both lay me down in peace, and sleep: for thou, Lord, only makest me dwell in safety. (Psalm 4:8)

> He that dwelleth in the secret place of the most High shall abide under the shadow of the Almighty. (Psalm 91:1)

> Blessed is the man that endureth temptation: for when he is tried, he shall receive the crown of life, which the Lord hath promised to them that love him. (James 1:12)

God is not about love. God is love.

> Wisdom is the principal thing; therefore get wisdom: and with all thy getting get understanding. (Proverbs 4:7)

Being unselfish will get you unstuck.
You are God's poem. You are a work of art. You are unique. There is nobody like you!

> And now these three remain: faith, hope and love. But the greatest of these is love. (1 Corinthians 13:13)

> Be strong and courageous. Do not be afraid
> or terrified because of them, for the Lord your
> God goes with you; he will never leave you nor
> forsake you. (Deuteronomy 31:6)

You will never have success if you are controlled by fear.

A person's virtue is often revealed by how gracefully they deal with adversity and disappointment.

Be comforted. Jesus will lead and defend you always. He's doing it today!

> The plans of the diligent lead to profit as
> surely as haste leads to poverty. (Proverbs 21:5)

> To do what is right and just is more accept-
> able to the Lord than sacrifice. (Proverbs 21:3)

> Whoever pursues righteousness and love
> finds life, prosperity and honor. (Proverbs 21:21)

Don't be upset for what you have lost. What God is going to release in your life is much greater than what you lost. You don't need anything you lost to bless you. Your crisis is a setup for the glory of God.

> And it shall come to pass, that whosoever
> shall call on the name of the Lord shall be saved.
> (Acts 2:21)

So give thanks to God today, for the Lord is good. His love extends to the ends of the earth and endures forever.

> Be completely humble and gentle; be patient,
> bearing with one another in love. (Ephesians 4:2)

One key to success is to build on your strengths so that your weaknesses become irrelevant.

Rest in the assurance that the Lord will take care of you.

The everlasting God is your shepherd; you shall not want.

> For His divine power has bestowed on us everything necessary for life and godliness, through true and personal knowledge of Him who called us by His own glory and excellence. (2 Peter 1:3)

Know your strengths. Know your weaknesses. Consider the capabilities God has given you.

Delay is not denial. God will answer your prayers at the perfect time.

The little things set up the big things.

Excuses comforts incapacity.

> The Lord is close to the brokenhearted and saves those who are crushed in spirit. (Psalm 34:18)

"You hold in your hand. You never left my side. And though my heart is torn. I will praise You in this storm" (Casting Crowns).

> I can do all things through Christ which strengtheneth me. (Philippians 4:13)

> When your problems of life knock you down get up dust yourself off and move forward. (Esther Wilson)

> Don't look to the left or the right at the problems around you just look up. (Marty Cerasoli)

Just keep it moving forward. (Lacinda Cerasoli)

The same thing that brings the curse brings the blessing. (T. D. Jakes)

I am blessed because I am the child of the King of kings, the heir of the Most High God. My life is blessed by the One who created everything. I am under the protection of the Almighty God who causes the earth to turn on its axis!

The reason you have value is because of what God says about you, not because of what other people say about you.

God has loved you with an everlasting love. No matter what you've done, he will always love you. That's passion!

To everything there is a season, and a time to every purpose under the heaven: A time to be born, and a time to die; a time to plant, and a time to pluck up that which is planted. (Ecclesiastes 3:1–2)

A time to weep, and a time to laugh; a time to mourn, and a time to dance. (Ecclesiastes 3:4)

And now abideth faith, hope, charity, these three; but the greatest of these is charity. (1 Corinthians 13:13)

You have a choice: Will you humble yourself, or will you live in arrogant, prideful denial? Will you be teachable or unreachable? God is for you, and he'll support you as you learn humility.

Our soul desires to be understanding, our ego is only concerned with being understood. When you are being understanding you are connected to your soul. (Michaiel Bovenes)

A gentle answer turns away wrath, but a
harsh word stirs up anger. (Proverbs 15:1)

Discover God's blueprint for you! God shaped you in a marvel-
ously unique way to fulfill a specific purpose here on earth.

You can't give up. I tell people be happy. Just
be happy. It's a choice. Things can be hard and
you just want to curl up but you have to shine.
(Ami Brown)

Worrying about it only makes it worse.
There is hope and that hope is having faith in
God. (Ami Brown)

It's not how you started in life; it's how you finish.
God remembered us when we were down; His love never quits.
Rescued us from the trampling boot, His love never quits. Takes care
of everyone in time of need, His love never quits. Thank God who
did it all! His love never quits!

"We should certainly count our blessings,
but we should also make our blessings count"
(Neal Maxwell).

Seeking happiness in God is the only method that provides
long-term happiness.

He who is generous will be blessed, for he
gives some of his food to the poor. (Proverbs
22:9)

Love never gives up, never loses faith, is
always hopeful, and endures through every cir-
cumstance. (1 Corinthians 13:7)

Whenever you compare yourself with others, you become discontent.

No matter what you face in life, you can take comfort in the fact that God is always with you.

> Do the best you can until you know better. Then when you know better, do better. (Maya Angelou).

> A calm and peaceful and tranquil heart is life and health to the body, but passion and envy are like rottenness to the bones. (Proverbs 14:30)

Thank you, Father, that we are reminded of the great mystery you have revealed to us in Jesus. Thank you for your love that sent Him to become our Savior, Lord, and King. In His name we pray. Amen.

Satan is constantly battling for your mind. That's where the battle happens. When God gives us an idea, it's an inspiration. When the devil gives us an idea, it's a temptation. You choose every day which thought you're going to dwell on.

> Accept God's salvation as your helmet, and take the sword of the Spirit, which is the word of God. (Ephesians 6:17)

> God is faithful; he will not let you be tempted beyond what you can bear. But when you are tempted, he will also provide a way out so that you can endure it. (1 Corinthians 10:13)

The happiest people in the world are those who hang on to what God says and follow it, regardless of what their feelings say.

> Let your light so shine before men, that they may see your good works, and glorify your Father which is in heaven. (Matthew 5:16)

Peace requires forgiveness.

> Thoughtless words can wound as deeply
> as any sword, but wisely spoken words can heal.
> (Proverbs 12:18)

Patience and prudence and wisdom are important in all our dealings with others.

Life is full of irritations, and a fool shows his annoyance at once. He easily flies off the handle. A prudent person rides above the surge of irritation and overlooks the provocation. Having a calm spirit is so important in raising children, in working with others, in race relations, in marriage, in international relationships—in fact, in all of life.

> Fools show their annoyance at once, but the
> prudent overlook an insult. (Proverbs 12:16)

Know that with a word, a thoughtful gesture, or simply a smile, you can bless another person!

You always lose when you give up your integrity.

> It is better to be poor and honest than to be
> foolish and tell lies. (Proverbs 19:1)

> For I, the Lord your God, will hold your
> right hand, Saying to you, "Fear not, I will help
> you." (Isaiah 41:13)

> Fear not, for I am with you; Be not dismayed, for I am your God. I will strengthen you,
> Yes, I will help you, I will uphold you with My
> righteous right hand. (Isaiah 41:10)

> And we know that all things work together
> for good to them that love God, to them who are
> the called according to his purpose. (Romans 8:28)

It's easier to maintain a good attitude and harder to get your good attitude back.

Welcome the last-minute changes that you encounter today with joy and gratefulness. Keep your eyes on the Lord, on His plan. Though it may not be what you imagine, it is, without a shadow of a doubt, the very best for you!

This day is a gift! It is whatever you decide to make of it. Your attitude today can keep you in God's peace or distance you from it.

If you don't live a life of love, then nothing you say will matter, nothing you know will matter, nothing you believe will matter, and nothing you give will matter.

> Many are the plans in the mind of a man,
> but it is the purpose of the Lord that will stand.
> (Proverbs 19:21)

> The heart of man plans his way, but the Lord establishes his steps. (Proverbs 16:9)

Even in the darkest night, God is the one who enlightens and guides you.

> For if ye forgive men their trespasses, your heavenly Father will also forgive you. (Matthew 6:14)

> Our Father which art in heaven, Hallowed be thy name. Thy kingdom come. Thy will be done in earth, as it is in heaven. Give us this day our daily bread. And forgive us our debts, as we forgive our debtors. And lead us not into temptation, but deliver us from evil: For thine is the kingdom, and the power, and the glory, for ever. Amen. (The Lord's Prayer, Matthew 6:9–13)

Blessed are the pure in heart: for they shall see God. (Matthew 5:8)

Let your light so shine before men, that they may see your good works, and glorify your Father which is in heaven. (Matthew 5:16)

Whenever you are able, do good to people who need help. (Proverbs 3:27 NCV)

God gave you abilities, talents, and energy to help other people.

Let us not be weary in well doing: for in due season we shall reap, if we faint not. (Galatians 6:9)

Lord, thank You that Your Word is perfect and unchanging. What You promise is guaranteed. I hold on to the beautiful promise of eternal life with You! In Jesus's name. Amen.

At the end of the day, tell yourself gently: I love you, you did the best you could today, and even if you didn't accomplish all you had planned, I love you anyway. (Anonymous).

He hath made the earth by his power, he hath established the world by his wisdom, and hath stretched out the heavens by his discretion. (Jeremiah 10:12)

Therefore being justified by faith, we have peace with God through our Lord Jesus Christ by whom also we have access by faith into this grace wherein we stand, and rejoice in hope of the glory of God. (Romans 5:1–2)

Lord, you remind us in your Word that because of all that Christ Jesus has done for us, we can give thanks in all circumstances. May our songs of praise and all our celebrations be acceptable to You. In Jesus's name, we pray. Amen.

Create in me a pure heart, O God, and renew a steadfast spirit within me. (Psalm 51:10)

Have mercy on me, O God, according to your unfailing love; according to your great compassion blot out my transgressions. (Psalm 51:1)

I lift up my eyes to the hills. From where does my help come? My help comes from the LORD, who made heaven and earth. (Psalm 121:1–2)

Father, Son, and Holy Spirit, Lord, I love You. Christ, I love You. Holy Spirit, I love You.

Be still, and know that I am God: I will be exalted among the heathen, I will be exalted in the earth. (Psalm 46:10)

The heart of man plans his way, but the Lord establishes his steps. (Proverbs 16:9)

This, then, is how you should pray: "Our Father in heaven, hallowed be your name, your kingdom come, your will be done, on earth as it is in heaven. Give us today our daily bread. And forgive us our debts, as we also have forgiven our debtors. And lead us not into temptation, but deliver us from the evil one." (Matthew 6:9–13)

And the Lord shall be king over all the earth:
in that day shall there be one Lord, and his name
one. (Zechariah 14:9)

God's Masterpiece

Whether you love or don't, love what you see in the mirror; you are God's masterpiece! You are His creation, and He has never and will never regret making you.

Faith and Endurance

By faith and endurance, you will enter into the inheritance that was promised to you by *God*.

But Jesus beheld them, and said unto them,
with men this is impossible; but with God all
things are possible. (Matthew 19:26)

Who is wise and understanding among
you? Let them show it by their good life, by deeds
done in the humility that comes from wisdom.
(James 3:13)

Actions Speak Louder Than Words

But someone will say, "You have faith; I have
deeds." Show me your faith without deeds, and I
will show you my faith by my deeds. (James 2:18)

As the body without the spirit is dead, so
faith without deeds is dead. (James 2:26)

Jesus answered, "I am the way and the truth
and the life. No one comes to the Father except
through me." (John 14:6)

Yet if any man suffer as a Christian, let him not be ashamed; but let him glorify God on this behalf. (1 Peter 4:16)

In God I will praise his word, in God I have put my trust; I will not fear what flesh can do unto me. (Psalm 56:4)

Oh, taste and see that the Lord is good; blessed is the man who trusts in Him! (Psalm 34:8)

God Never Tires of You

God will never have "enough" of you. You don't bore *Him*, and *He* doesn't tire of you. You are His beloved daughter, His beloved son!

The eyes of the Lord are on the righteous, and His ears are open to their cry. (Psalm 34:8)

Jesus said to him, "I am the way, and the truth, and the life. No one comes to the Father except through me." (John 14:6)

For the wages of sin is death, but the gift of God is eternal life in Christ Jesus our Lord. (Romans 6:2)

In the same way, let your light shine before others, that they may see your good deeds and glorify your Father in heaven. (Matthew 5: 16)

Not only so, but we also glory in our sufferings, because we know that suffering produces perseverance; perseverance, character; and character, hope. (Romans 5:3–4)

Blessed be the God and Father of our Lord Jesus Christ, the Father of compassion and the God of all comfort, who comforts us in all our troubles, so that we can comfort those in any trouble with the comfort we ourselves have received from God. For just as the sufferings of Christ overflow to us, so also through Christ our comfort overflows. (2 Corinthians 1:3–5)

Rescue me, O Lord, from my enemies; I take refuge in You. (Psalm 143:9)

Let me hear Your lovingkindness in the morning, for I trust in You. Teach me the way in which I should walk, for I lift up my soul to You. (Psalm 143:8)

Search me, O God, and know my heart: try me, and know my thoughts: And see if there be any wicked way in me, and lead me in the way everlasting. (Psalms 139:23–24)

Bless and show kindness to those who curse you, pray for those who mistreat you. (Luke 6:28)

For the word of God is living and active and full of power [making it operative, energizing, and effective]. It is sharper than any two-edged sword, penetrating as far as the division of the soul and spirit [the completeness of a person], and of both joints and marrow [the deepest parts of our nature], exposing and judging the very thoughts and intentions of the heart. (Hebrews 4:12)

Do not be overcome by evil, but overcome evil with good. (Romans 12:21)

And this is the confidence that we have in him, that, if we ask anything according to his will, he heareth us: And if we know that he hear us, whatsoever we ask, we know that we have the petitions that we desired of him. (1 John 5:14–15)

Better is little with the fear of the Lord than great treasure and trouble therewith. (Proverbs 15:16)

Closer to Jesus

The closer you get to Jesus, the more you will learn just how valuable you truly are. In turn, you stop accepting unacceptable behavior as "normal."

Courage

Courage is what will change your life. And courage is not the absence of fear but, instead, moving forward despite fear.

With God

With God's help, you can overcome every difficulty and obstacle no matter what it is.

Moving toward God

When you move toward fulfilling God's dream for your life, you will encounter obstacles, battles, and suffering, but nothing in heaven or on earth can stop you!

God's True Love

God didn't give up on Israel, and he doesn't give up on us either. No matter the disrespect and dishonor we have shown, God still loves us and strives to win us back. The false gods of the world require people to pursue them, but the true God of love pursues us.

God's Love

God is such a loving father that it's hard to imagine a human being ever showing Him the honor He deserves. God is such a gracious and kind master that it's hard to imagine a human able to repay Him the respect that is due Him. And yet God does not give up His love for us. Romans 5:8 says, "God demonstrates his own love for us in this: While we were still sinners, Christ died for us."

Helping a Person in Need

God will have you help a person in need to help you more than you think.

> The night is far spent, the day is at hand: let us therefore cast off the works of darkness, and let us put on the armour of light. (Romans 13:12)

> "Though the mountains be shaken and the hills be removed, yet my unfailing love for you will not be shaken nor my covenant of peace be removed," says the LORD, who has compassion on you. (Isaiah 54:10)

> Be not hasty in thy spirit to be angry: for anger resteth in the bosom of fools. (Ecclesiastes 7:9 KJV)

Fix the Problem

Fix the problem, not the blame. You need to learn to attack the issue, not each other. The blame game is a waste of time. Anytime you're busy fixing blame, you're wasting energy and not fixing the problem.

Ask God for Wisdom

God's wisdom is there for you. Ask Him. Consult Him. He will answer you. God wants you to succeed because He loves you!

You Belong to God

You belong to God. He loves you. He allows circumstances you can't escape from only to draw you closer to Him.

> These things I have spoken unto you, that in me ye might have peace. In the world ye shall have tribulation: but be of good cheer; I have overcome the world. (John 16:33)

> Peace I leave with you, my peace I give unto you: not as the world giveth, give I unto you. Let not your heart be troubled, neither let it be afraid. (John 14:27)

> Delight thyself also in the LORD: and he shall give thee the desires of thine heart. (Psalms 37:4)

> Just as charcoal and wood keep a fire going, a quarrelsome person keeps an argument going. (Proverbs 26:21)

Don't Get Sucked In

Somebody once said, "If you wrestle in the mud with a pig, both of you will get dirty, but only one of you will enjoy it." Stay out of the mud. Don't get sucked into the argument. Just walk on by.

Control Your Thoughts

Satan gives you thoughts; they are temptation. And God gives you thoughts; they are inspiration. Which are you going to choose? Romans 8:6 (NIV) says, "The mind of sinful man is death, but the mind controlled by the Spirit is life and peace."

How much do you love yourself?

We love others the way we love ourselves.

No Parking at Any Time

Don't park at the point of your pain. Keep moving forward in faith. God will not reject you.

> Trust in him at all times; ye people, pour
> out your heart before him: God is a refuge for us.
> Selah. (Psalm 62:8 KJV)

God Knows What You Need

Never run after people who God removed from your life to protect you. Trust in God. He will bring the right people in your life because He knows exactly who you need.

> Delight thyself also in the LORD: and he
> shall give thee the desires of thine heart. (Psalm
> 37:4)

Gossip

> You will keep your friends if you forgive them, but you will lose your friends if you keep talking about what they did wrong. (Proverbs 17:9 CEV)

> Make allowance for each other's faults, and forgive anyone who offends you. Remember, the Lord forgave you, so you must forgive others. (Colossians 3:13)

> Be patient with each other, making allowance for each other's faults because of your love. (Ephesians 4:2b TLB)

Do you think being rich without God will give you a better life? Without God, you are just a poor person with lots of money.

God gives other people talent for us to enjoy not to be jealous of. Don't wish you had someone else's talent; the gift God gave you is great.

Putting your faith in God is the answer for your fear. If you move with God. God will move with you.

Our vision gets better when we are older in God not in the world. The more you allow God to guide you, *His* plan for you will become clearer.

A lot of the times, tests in our lives come before a great blessing.

Don't let someone's opinions dictate your life. Let the Lord guide your life.

Sometimes God will place us where we don't want to be. Have you thought that maybe God wants you to rest and trust in *Him*? Walk in faith; God loves you and will not leave you.

> There is never a time that God is not blessing his children. (Brother Andrew Rolle)

Always remember God will always be with you because *He* is faithful. God will allow awkward moments in your life to have you grow.

Having faith is not emotional. It's deciding to live by God's word.

Always know that Jesus is your peace in this crazy world.

Trusting in God even when you don't understand *His* plan is walking in faith.

Until you truly forgive the person that hurt you, you will always be bound to that person.

If you can't be yourself or not allowed to be yourself in a relationship, then maybe that person is not the one the Lord has for you.

Works of the flesh will always lead to frustration. Ask God for guidance and wisdom.

There is nothing that you have done in the past that God will not forgive. All you have to do is ask.

Ain't no party like a Holy Ghost party. (Pastor George Stephens)

Stress comes from trying to do everything on your own. Peace comes from putting it all in God's hands. (Unknown)

And whatever things you ask in prayer, believing, you will receive. (Matthew 21:22)

God has a plan for your life. You may have changed in your lifetime, but God's love for you will never change.

If you leave everything in God's hands. You will start to see God's hands in everything.

No matter how much a person has hurt you or has done you wrong, do not hate them.

Always be humble no matter how rich you have become.

No matter what the devil throws your way, stand strong in faith; God will get you through it.

Love yourself, and never think you are alone; God is with you. Always pray; God listens.

Make your decisions through God's will, not by your emotions.

The devil uses the negative thoughts in our minds as his own dumpster. Put on the armor of God.

We were born into inherited sin. Yet as we get older, we choose to live in sin which is not inherited.

How long will you dwell in what you have lost? Dwelling in your lost delays what great new blessings the Lord has in store for you.

Always keep your eyes on Jesus, and do one thing at a time.

Do not throw stones that people throw at you back at them. Use them to build the path to your own success.

While you are in a bad place, have faith, and look for something good.

You will never know if you're doing something right if you are afraid of doing something wrong.

> Set a guard over my mouth, Lord; keep
> watch over the door of my lips. (Psalm 141:3)

Always trust in the Lord no matter what difficulties come your way.

If you want to have positive and good people around you, then you should be positive, and be good to people also.

> Waiting is a sign of true love and patience.
> Anyone can say I love you, but not anyone
> can wait and prove it's true. (Matt Mcmillen
> Ministries)

If you are going through a rough time, it may not be your fault, *but* it is your fault if you dwell in your rough time.

Don't let people that hurt you take your self-control. Stand fast, and let it go.

We always trust God in the light, but do we always trust God in the dark?

Commit thy works unto the LORD, and thy
thoughts shall be established. (Proverbs 16:3)

There is no liberation in revenge. Put it in God's hands, and *He*
will handle it for you.

Why do we complain about things that happen on a daily basis
instead of thanking the Lord for the things we have and can do?

Being aggressive looking for peace is a good thing when you do
it through the Lord.

Be yourself! Everybody else is taken! (Joyce
Myers)

The things we buy wear out and become outdated, but the
word of Lord never has and never will wear out or become outdated.

Everything you do, do it unto the Lord.

Do you use the blessings from God to help people, or do you
use people to get things and claim it was a blessing?

You will go so much further working with faith in the Lord
rather than no faith at all. Working in faith is much better than
working without faith at all.

"The devil wants you to worry about your future so you can't
enjoy your life right now. The devil is a *liar*! Enjoy every minute of
your life because it's a gift from God" (God Seekers).

Anyone who listens to my teaching and fol-
lows it is wise, like a person who builds a house
on solid rock. (Matthew 7:24 NLT)

The only way you can truly love someone is to love yourself
first.

The more time you spend with God, your joy and peace will
increase, and you become a stronger person.

Don't say you can't find the time for prayer. Make the time for
prayer. Thank God for the blessings in your life.

Don't only seek God when you are desperate. Seek God all the time.

Don't put God around your schedule. Put your schedule around God. Keep God first in your life.

God made you to be original. Don't compare yourself to others. Just simply be yourself.

Ask God to give you strength to step out of your comfort zone. Stepping out of your comfort zone with the Lord will bring growth in your life.

Stop thinking of what you are not. Start thinking of what you have become. Enjoy your life with the Lord.

Managing your thoughts and attitude while waiting on God's answer is the key to your joy.

God puts everyone in your life for a reason, either it's for a blessing or a lesson. But know it's meant for you to grow into a better person.

If you are in a time of struggle, don't give up hope. You are not failing; you are growing.

No matter how hard it gets or how painful it is, know that God will get you through it.

Don't ever think praying is a waste of time when you don't get what you prayed for. In fact, you lose when you pray and have faith. You lose stress, anger, greed, depression, and hate.

If you quit in the middle of something, you will never get to the end. Stay focused and have faith; God will lead you through it.

When someone mistreats you, it's not your fault. There is nothing wrong with you. There is something wrong with them.

Even though life is not fair at times and people have caused you pain, know the God is just and will make things right.

When things don't go as planned, God will eventually reveal *His* plan for you. So have faith and enjoy your journey.

Being poor does not mean you have no money. Being poor means you don't have Christ in your life.

God knew before you were born that you would be reading this in this moment. He planned to get your attention for just a few seconds so he could say this to you: I've seen every hurt in your life, and I've never stopped loving you. You matter to me. I love you more than you will ever know. I made you to love you, and I've been waiting for you to love me back.

> Therefore the Lord himself shall give you a sign; Behold, a virgin shall conceive, and bear a son, and shall call his name Immanuel. (Isaiah 7:14)

Father, thank You for the things that You have prepared for those who love You. I love You with my whole heart. And I pray that today, Your Spirit, which is a Spirit of revelation, shows and reveals to me these things that are prepared in advance. I want to receive them, and I will because I know that You want the best for my life! In Jesus's name. Amen.

> For I reckon that the sufferings of this present time are not worthy to be compared with the glory which shall be revealed in us. (Romans 8:18)

God wants you to remember that He is faithful, always present with you, and that nothing could ever change that. He was, is, and always will be your Father.

You need to live for an audience of one: God. That's Jesus's path to complete and total joy. He said,

> I have told you this so that my joy may be in you and that your joy may be complete. (John 15:11)

> But seek ye first the kingdom of God, and his righteousness; and all these things shall be added unto you. (Matthew 6:33)

> There is none holy as the Lord: for there is none beside thee: neither is there any rock like our God. (1 Samuel 2:2)

A righteous man of God would offer a weary traveler a bed for the night and invite him to share a quiet conversation of the Lord over a bowl of soup.

It's not about anger; it's about peace. It's not about power; it's about grace. It's not about knowing your enemy; it's about knowing yourself.

Storms may rage, but they are but for a moment. Your God's favor is for life!

> The Lord shall fight for you, and ye shall hold your peace. (Exodus 14:14)

> He that followeth after righteousness and mercy findeth life, righteousness, and honour. (Proverbs 21:21)

> What shall we then say to these things? If God be for us, who can be against us? (Romans 8:31)

I will praise thee, O Lord, with my whole heart; I will shew forth all thy marvellous works. (Psalms 9:1)

O Lord, thou art my God; I will exalt thee, I will praise thy name; for thou hast done wonderful things; thy counsels of old are faithfulness and truth. (Isaiah 25:1)

Because thy lovingkindness is better than life, my lips shall praise thee. 4 Thus will I bless thee while I live: I will lift up my hands in thy name. (Psalm 63:3–4)

People may not remember what you said but will remember how you made them feel.

Love a person for the way they are and not the way you want them to be.

Thanks be unto God for his unspeakable gift. (2 Corinthians 9:15)

But thanks be to God, which giveth us the victory through our Lord Jesus Christ. (1 Corinthians 15:57)

Now therefore, our God, we thank thee, and praise thy glorious name. (1 Chronicles 29:13)

For the grace of God that bringeth salvation hath appeared to all men, teaching us that, denying ungodliness and worldly lusts, we should live soberly, righteously, and godly, in this present world; (Titus 2:11–12)

Be not deceived; God is not mocked: for whatsoever a man soweth, that shall he also reap. For he that soweth to his flesh shall of the flesh reap corruption; but he that soweth to the Spirit shall of the Spirit reap life everlasting. (Galatians 6:7–8)

For the earth shall be filled with the knowledge of the glory of the Lord, as the waters cover the sea. (Habakkuk 2:14)

Walk in wisdom toward them that are without, redeeming the time. Let your speech be always with grace, seasoned with salt, that ye may know how ye ought to answer every man. (Colossians 4:5–6)

He that keepeth his mouth keepeth his life: but he that openeth wide his lips shall have destruction. (Proverbs 13:3)

Courage is contagious. You never know how many people will join you until you courageously step out in faith.
If we chase God, *His* blessings will chase us.

Walk with the wise and become wise, for a companion of fools suffers harm. (Proverbs 13:20)

Verily, verily, I say unto you, He that heareth my word, and believeth on him that sent me, hath everlasting life, and shall not come into condemnation; but is passed from death unto life. (John 5:24)

We must feed our faith with the promises of *God*.

> May the grace of the Lord Jesus Christ, and the love of God, and the fellowship of the Holy Spirit be with you all. (2 Corinthians 13:14)

Don't be ashamed of who you are. Don't apologize for existing! Instead, why not choose to thank God for who you are?

You are absolutely unique, and no one else but you can be *you*! Learn to appreciate yourself as you are, with your strengths and even your flaws! Yes, because what God is perfecting in you is an opportunity for Him to support and transform you by His Spirit.

The challenge for us is twofold: We must not allow others to make us feel negatively about ourselves. But we also must make sure that we do not make others feel inferior to us. Treat others like the children of God as well. It's not about being superior; it's about being godlike.

Sadly, people will often try to make you feel inferior for a variety of reasons: to make themselves feel superior, to win, or out of fear of being judged themselves. But God claims each of us as his very own. You are not inferior. You are a child of God, and no one has the right to treat you any other way!

> Wherefore thou art great, O Lord God: for there is none like thee, neither is there any God beside thee, according to all that we have heard with our ears. (2 Samuel 7:22)

> Wherefore, my beloved brethren, let every man be swift to hear, slow to speak, slow to wrath: (James 1:19)

> And let the peace of God rule in your hearts, to the which also ye are called in one body; and be ye thankful. (Colossians 3:15)

*B*ought by the blood of Jesus

*L*iving in His victory

*E*stablished in faith

*S*aved from the curse of sin, despair, depression, and death

*S*ecure in the knowledge of His forgiveness and faithfulness

*E*xpectant that good things will happen today

*D*elivered to bring deliverance!

Simply put, a life without Christ has no worth. It means eternal death and damnation.

Knowing Christ brings righteousness.

Now the Lord is that Spirit: and where the Spirit of the Lord is, there is liberty. (2 Corinthians 3:17)

A man's heart deviseth his way: but the Lord directeth his steps. (Proverbs 16:9)

I will both lay me down in peace, and sleep: for thou, Lord, only makest me dwell in safety. (Psalms 4:8)

He that dwelleth in the secret place of the most High shall abide under the shadow of the Almighty. (Psalms 91:1)

> Blessed is the man that endureth temptation: for when he is tried, he shall receive the crown of life, which the Lord hath promised to them that love him. (James 1:12)

God is not about love. God is love.

> Wisdom is the principal thing; therefore get wisdom: and with all thy getting get understanding. (Proverbs 4:7)

Being unselfish will get you unstuck.

You are God's poem. You are a work of art. You are unique. There is nobody like you!

> And now these three remain: faith, hope and love. But the greatest of these is love. (1 Corinthians 13:13)

> Be strong and courageous. Do not be afraid or terrified because of them, for the Lord your God goes with you; he will never leave you nor forsake you. (Deuteronomy 31:6)

You will never have success if you are controlled by fear.

A person's virtue is often revealed by how gracefully they deal with disappointment.

Be comforted. Jesus will lead and defend you always. He's doing it today!

> The plans of the diligent lead to profit as surely as haste leads to poverty. (Proverbs 21:5)

> To do what is right and just is more acceptable to the Lord than sacrifice. (Proverbs 21:3)

> Whoever pursues righteousness and love
> finds life, prosperity and honor. (Proverbs 21:21)

Don't be upset for what you have lost. What God is going to release in your life is much greater than what you lost. You don't need anything you lost to bless you.

Your crisis is a setup for the glory of God.

> And it shall come to pass, that whosoever
> shall call on the name of the Lord shall be saved.
> (Acts 2:21)

So give thanks to God today, for the Lord is good. His love extends to the ends of the earth and endures forever.

> Be completely humble and gentle; be
> patient, bearing with one another in love.
> (Ephesians 4:2)

One key to success is to build on your strengths so that your weaknesses become irrelevant.

Rest in the assurance that the Lord will take care of you.

The everlasting God is your shepherd; you shall not want.

> For His divine power has bestowed on
> us everything necessary for life and godliness,
> through true and personal knowledge of Him
> who called us by His own glory and excellence.
> (2 Peter 1:3)

Know your strengths. Know your weaknesses. Consider the capabilities God has given you.

Delay is not denial. God will answer your prayers at the perfect time.

The little things set up the big things.

Excuses comforts incapacity.

> The Lord is close to the brokenhearted and saves those who are crushed in spirit. (Psalm 34:18)

> You hold in Your hand. You never left my side. And though my heart is torn. I will praise You in this storm. (Casting Crowns)

God is not about love. God is love.

> Wisdom is the principal thing; therefore get wisdom: and with all thy getting get understanding. (Proverbs 4:7)

Being unselfish will get you unstuck.
You are God's poem. You are a work of art. You are unique. There is nobody like you!

> And now these three remain: faith, hope and love. But the greatest of these is love. (1 Corinthians 13:13)

> Be strong and courageous. Do not be afraid or terrified because of them, for the Lord your God goes with you; he will never leave you nor forsake you. (Deuteronomy 31:6)

You will never have success if you are controlled by fear.
A person's virtue is often revealed by how gracefully they deal with disappointment.
Be comforted. Jesus will lead and defend you always. He's doing it today!

> The plans of the diligent lead to profit as surely as haste leads to poverty. (Proverbs 21:5)

To do what is right and just is more acceptable to the Lord than sacrifice. (Proverbs 21:3)

Whoever pursues righteousness and love
finds life, prosperity and honor. (Proverbs 21:21)

Don't be upset for what you have lost. What God is going to
release in your life is much greater than what you lost. You don't need
anything you lost to bless you.

Your crisis is a setup for the glory of God.

And it shall come to pass, that whosoever
shall call on the name of the Lord shall be saved.
(Acts 2:21)

So give thanks to God today, for the Lord is good. His love
extends to the ends of the earth and endures forever.

Be completely humble and gentle; be
patient, bearing with one another in love.
(Ephesians 4:2)

One key to success is to build on your strengths so that your
weaknesses become irrelevant.

Rest in the assurance that the Lord will take care of you.

The everlasting God is your shepherd; you shall not want.

For His divine power has bestowed on
us everything necessary for life and godliness,
through true and personal knowledge of Him
who called us by His own glory and excellence.
(2 Peter 1:3)

Know your strengths. Know your weaknesses. Consider the
capabilities God has given you.

Delay is not denial. God will answer your prayers at the perfect
time.

The little things set up the big things.
Excuses comforts incapacity.

> The Lord is close to the brokenhearted and
> saves those who are crushed in spirit. (Psalm
> 34:18)

> You hold in Your hand. You never left my
> side. And though my heart is torn. I will praise
> You in this storm. (Casting Crowns).

One key to success is to build on your strengths so that your
weaknesses become irrelevant.
Rest in the assurance that the Lord will take care of you.
The everlasting God is your shepherd; you shall not want.

> For His divine power has bestowed on
> us everything necessary for life and godliness,
> through true and personal knowledge of Him
> who called us by His own glory and excellence.
> (2 Peter 1:3)

Know your strengths. Know your weaknesses. Consider the
capabilities God has given you.
Delay is not denial. God will answer you prayers at the perfect
time.
The little things set up the big things.
Excuses comforts incapacity.

> Blessed are the meek: for they shall inherit
> the earth. (Matthew 5:5)

> By whom also we have access by faith into
> this grace wherein we stand, and rejoice in hope
> of the glory of God. (Romans 5:2)

Lord, you remind us in your Word that because of all that Christ Jesus has done for us, we can give thanks in all circumstances. May our songs of praise and all our celebrations be acceptable to You. In Jesus's name we pray. Amen.

> Create in me a pure heart, O God, and renew a steadfast spirit within me. (Psalm 51:10)

> You can actually isolate yourself from God in your own thoughts and actions until you hear nothing but silence. Then you just realize how numb and alone you have become. (Lacinda Ceresoli)

Value yourself in Christ. Love yourself, and know that God is with you.

Complaining while feeling lonely? Use the time alone to get closer to God.

Don't let how people treat you to determine your value. Know you are a child of God.

Ask God to use you to be a blessing to someone. Remember not only poor people need blessings; everyone needs a blessing.

It's our responsibility to be happy. Forgive others as quickly as they offend you.

In order to grow spiritually, one must love and forgive people and not get offended about everything.

A true man or woman of God has worth in his or her actions for the needs of others.

Hate your sin, but love yourself.

There are times that life is not fair, but know that God is just.

What spiritual gifts and talents has God given you that you can use to help others?

No matter how strong your temptation is, do your best to maintain your integrity with God.

How can you ask God to forgive you if you can't forgive others?

A single lie discovered is enough to create doubt in every truth expressed.

God loves you and wants you to be happy. It's your choice if you want to be happy.

Be content where you are at while you are on your way to where you are going.

Seek God even if you don't have a problem and not only when you have a problem. Love God with all your heart.

Sometimes your place of battle is your place of blessings. The Lord will use your battle ground to give you wisdom.

Stop looking at wrong places and people to fix your issues. Know that your mighty God will fix your issues. All you have to do is ask with great faith.

Don't look how far you have to go. Look how far you have come.

Joy is a gift from knowing God.

If it costs you your peace, it's too expensive. Pray for peace and wisdom.

God does not pressure us to make a decision. If you feel pressured to make a decision, it's not from God.

Do what God wants, not what people want.

God is always right, so when you disagree with God, you are wrong.

To forgive is to set a prisoner free and discover that the prisoner was us. Pray for wisdom.

Conflicts hurt and can leave emotional, even spiritual, scars. Sometimes, our first reaction is to cling to our anger and build a wall so we don't get hurt even more. But God, who is full of love, encourages us to let go. *He* is just, and *He* knows how to take care of us like no one else!

> He heals the brokenhearted and binds up
> their wounds. (Psalm 147:3)

The best thing you can do is be a light in someone else's darkness. Joy comes from helping others, not from getting what you want.

> Thank you, Lord, for everything you've
> done for me. Forgive me of all my sins. Be the

Lord of my life. Create in me a clean heart and the right spirit within me; renew my mind. Heal me from the hurt of my past. I love you and need you. Cover me with your precious and holy blood as well as my family, my friends, and my life projects. Give me your dream, Lord. Bless and protect everyone that seeks you, needs you, and believes in you. (Unknown).

You cannot have fear and faith at the same time. Put your faith in the Lord and watch *Him* fight your battles.

It's not my fight. It's God's fight. I do my best, and *He* takes care of the rest. (Dewyan Cerisoli)

Praying with a selfish heart does not get prayers answered.

When a person pass away, we let people know by putting the birthdate a dash and the date of passing. Let me ask you this: What did you do during your dash? The dash indicates your life, so what did you do during your dash? Did you help others, or did you live a selfish life? Are you living as an honorable person, or are you just trying to cheat people out of something that can help them? Will you be remembered as a great and caring person or as a person that did people wrong?

Live this new day with joy; breathe deeply. Stand up, and go for all the beautiful blessings that God has prepared exclusively for you from *His* love.

Expect the best from the best. That is why I expect the best from God since *He* is the best.

Don't you dare give up! Draw from the strength of God. At times, there are curses before blessings.

Ask for wisdom in the middle of your storm. Have faith God is with you.

How can you pray for something new if you don't appreciate what God has blessed you with?

Know this: the Lord's word is greater than any of your affliction. I can't thank God enough for all my blessings.

> In everything give thanks: for this is the
> will of God in Christ Jesus concerning you.
> (1 Thessalonians 5:18)

Your dreams will never move toward you. Put God first in your life, and move toward your dream.

Don't say, God is my copilot. Make *Him* your pilot in your life.

Be known by your faith not your beliefs.

Walking in obedience in the Lord brings humility.

Planning things in life are good. But we must remember that life goes by one day at a time. So have faith that the Lord will guide you one day at a time. All you've got to do is ask.

Just know that the storm is only temporary. God is eternal.

Jesus is in the midst of your storm and will rescue you. All you need to do is step out in the storm, and know that Jesus is in the storm with you.

Step over all the bad things in your life, and take a leap of faith in the Lord.

Jesus will walk through the danger zone to get you out of it. All it takes is faith.

The sin that God won't forgive is the one you don't ask forgiveness for.

Do not bury yourself in the past. Put God first, and let *Him* guide your future. That is why a rearview mirror is so small, and your windshield is big.

God does not allow pain in our lives without a purpose.

> "Silence can never be misunderstood. Walk
> by faith not by sight" (Pastor George Stephens).

Don't block your blessings by being jealous of someone else's blessing.

Don't ever think what you have lost was the best you ever had. God has the best in store for you. Be strong in faith.

God is a God of justice. He will make what's wrong right.

We always trust God in the light, but do we always trust God in the dark?

Commit thy works unto the LORD, and thy
thoughts shall be established. (Proverbs 16:3)

There is no liberation in revenge. Put it in God's hands, and *He* will handle it for you.

Even though life is not fair at times and people have caused you pain, know that God is just and will make things right.

When things don't go as planned, God will eventually reveal *His* plan for you. So have faith, and enjoy your journey.

About the Author

Pedro Wilson was born and raised in El Paso, Texas. He studied and trained in martial arts for over fifteen years in Denton, Texas at Reding Martial Arts and reached full instructor level in the Progressive Fighting System.

Pedro teach his students martial arts and the Word of God. He inspires his students to always put God first and believe that Jesus is the way of life.

CPSIA information can be obtained
at www.ICGtesting.com
Printed in the USA
BVHW041443300523
665026BV00001B/130